THIS JOURNAL BELONGS TO:

If you love our book cover, check out our design store (scan the code) to see this cover design on a range of products including stickers, notebooks and even duvet covers!

scan me!

Even Unicorns have Blah Days...

This little journal helps children identify and express feelings to encourage positivity, help manage anxiety and frustration, and generally promote wellbeing.

The deceptively simple design is based on scientifically proven methods that deliver powerful results through repetition. For example, knowing they will need to list the top three things at the end of the day encourages children to look for positive events, which develops a positive bias.

Designed to be used with minimal instruction, a daily entry should take just a few minutes to complete - we've provided an example at the start of the journal. The daily spreads are undated and can be used as frequently as desired though it is recommended to complete 5 days in a row when starting out. This journal also includes more detailed writing and drawing prompts every 5 entries to spark creativity and encourage deeper reflection.

We hope you find this journal fun and beneficial and when it's time to replace it, check out the other titles in the range by scanning the QR code below.

scan Me

M T W T (F) S S

Date: 9/9/2021

Three things I felt today:

1. Excitement
2. Happiness
3. Impatience

EXAMPLE

Today I mostly felt:

Draw how you felt on the unicorn's face

Did anything make me feel anxious, frustrated or sad? If so, why?

Today I didn't feel any of these things.

Top three things about today:

1. I went to my friend's party.
2. Eating birthday cake.
3. Playing with my friends.

Three things I'm grateful for today:

1. My mom for taking me to the party.
2. My friends.
3. Birthday cake!

This is my work of art   Date: _____

Date: _____

What do you think happiness means?

_____

_____

_____

_____

_____

_____

_____

_____

_____

_____

_____

_____

_____

_____

_____

_____

_____

M T W T F S S

Date: _____

Three things I felt today:

1. _____
2. _____
3. _____

Today I mostly felt:

Draw how you felt on the unicorn's face

Did anything make me feel anxious, frustrated or sad? If so, why?

_____
_____
_____
_____

Top three things about today:

1 _____
2 _____
3 _____

Three things I'm grateful for today:

1 _____
2 _____
3 _____

M T W T F S S

Date: _____

Three things I felt today:

1. _____
2. _____
3. _____

Today I mostly felt:

Draw how you felt on the unicorn's face

Did anything make me feel anxious, frustrated or sad? If so, why?

_____

_____

_____

_____

Top three things about today:

1 _____

2 _____

3 _____

Three things I'm grateful for today:

1 _____

2 _____

3 _____

M T W T F S S

Date: _____

Three things I felt today:

1. _____
2. _____
3. _____

Today I mostly felt:

Draw how you felt on the unicorn's face

Did anything make me feel anxious, frustrated or sad? If so, why?

_____

_____

_____

_____

_____

Top three things about today:

① _____

② _____

③ _____

Three things I'm grateful for today:

① _____

② _____

③ _____

M T W T F S S

Date: _____

Three things I felt today:

1
2
3

Today I mostly felt:

Draw how you felt on the unicorn's face

Did anything make me feel anxious, frustrated or sad? If so, why?

_____

_____

_____

_____

_____

Top three things about today:

1 _____

2 _____

3 _____

Three things I'm grateful for today:

1 _____

2 _____

3 _____

M T W T F S S

Date: _____

Three things I felt today:

1. _____
2. _____
3. _____

Today I mostly felt:

Draw how you felt on the unicorn's face

Did anything make me feel anxious, frustrated or sad? If so, why?

_____

_____

_____

_____

Top three things about today:

① _____

② _____

③ _____

Three things I'm grateful for today:

① _____

② _____

③ _____

This is my work of art   Date: _____

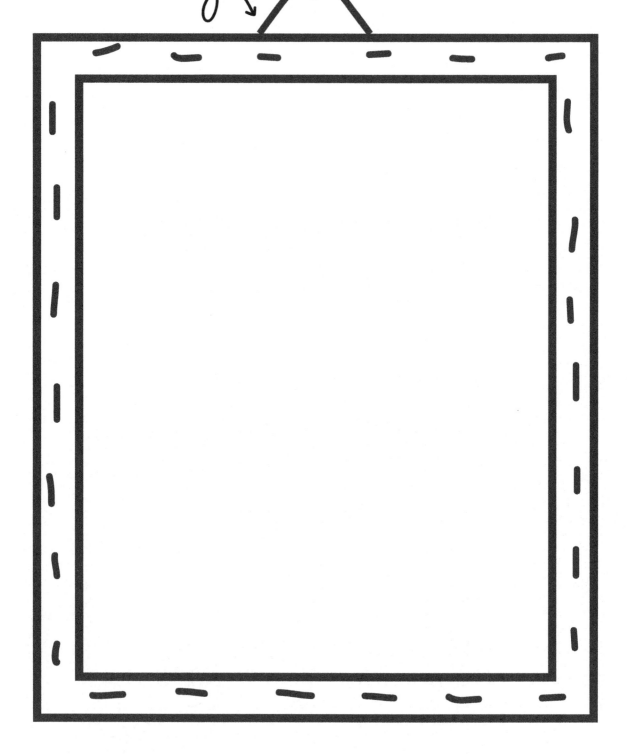

Date: _____

What does it mean to be a good friend?

_____

_____

_____

_____

_____

_____

_____

_____

_____

_____

_____

_____

_____

_____

_____

_____

_____

_____

M T W T F S S

Date: _____

Three things I felt today:

 _____

 _____

 _____

Today I mostly felt:

Draw how you felt on the unicorn's face

Did anything make me feel anxious, frustrated or sad? If so, why?

_____

_____

_____

_____

_____

Top three things about today:

① _____

② _____

③ _____

Three things I'm grateful for today:

① _____

② _____

③ _____

M T W T F S S

Date: _____

Three things I felt today:

① _____
② _____
③ _____

Today I mostly felt:

Draw how you felt on the unicorn's face

Did anything make me feel anxious, frustrated or sad? If so, why?

_____

_____

_____

_____

_____

Top three things about today:

1 _____

2 _____

3 _____

Three things I'm grateful for today:

1 _____

2 _____

3 _____

M T W T F S S

Date: _____

Three things I felt today:

① _____

② _____

③ _____

Today I mostly felt:

Draw how you felt on the unicorn's face

Did anything make me feel anxious, frustrated or sad? If so, why?

_____

_____

_____

_____

_____

Top three things about today:

(1) _____

(2) _____

(3) _____

Three things I'm grateful for today:

(1) _____

(2) _____

(3) _____

M T W T F S S

Date: _____

Three things I felt today:

① _____
② _____
③ _____

Today I mostly felt:

Draw how you felt on the unicorn's face

Did anything make me feel anxious, frustrated or sad? If so, why?

_____

_____

_____

_____

_____

Top three things about today:

1. _____
2. _____
3. _____

Three things I'm grateful for today:

1. _____
2. _____
3. _____

M T W T F S S

Date: _____

Three things I felt today:

1
2
3

Today I mostly felt:

Draw how you felt on the unicorn's face

Did anything make me feel anxious, frustrated or sad? If so, why?

_____

_____

_____

_____

_____

Top three things about today:

① _____

② _____

③ _____

Three things I'm grateful for today:

① _____

② _____

③ _____

This is my work of art   Date: _____

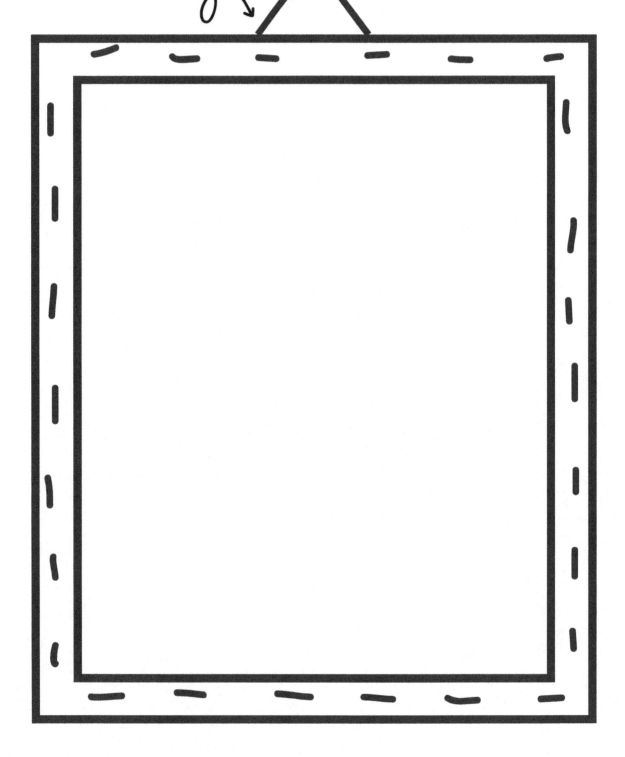

Date: _____

What is your favourite thing to do & why?

_____
_____
_____
_____
_____
_____
_____
_____
_____
_____
_____
_____
_____
_____
_____
_____
_____
_____

M T W T F S S

Date: _____

Three things I felt today:

 _____

 _____

 _____

Today I mostly felt:

Draw how you felt on the unicorn's face

Did anything make me feel anxious, frustrated or sad? If so, why?

_____

_____

_____

_____

_____

Top three things about today:

(1) _____

(2) _____

(3) _____

Three things I'm grateful for today:

(1) _____

(2) _____

(3) _____

M T W T F S S

Date: _____

Three things I felt today:

1.
2.
3.

Today I mostly felt:

Draw how you felt on the unicorn's face

Did anything make me feel anxious, frustrated or sad? If so, why?

_____
_____
_____
_____
_____

Top three things about today:

① _____
② _____
③ _____

Three things I'm grateful for today:

① _____
② _____
③ _____

M T W T F S S

Date: _____

Three things I felt today:

1. _____
2. _____
3. _____

Today I mostly felt:

Draw how you felt on the unicorn's face

Did anything make me feel anxious, frustrated or sad? If so, why?

_____

_____

_____

_____

Top three things about today:

(1) _____

(2) _____

(3) _____

Three things I'm grateful for today:

(1) _____

(2) _____

(3) _____

M T W T F S S

Date: _____

Three things I felt today:

① _____
② _____
③ _____

Today I mostly felt:

Draw how you felt on the unicorn's face

Did anything make me feel anxious, frustrated or sad? If so, why?

_____

_____

_____

_____

Top three things about today:

① _____

② _____

③ _____

Three things I'm grateful for today:

① _____

② _____

③ _____

M T W T F S S

Date: _____

Three things I felt today:

1. _____
2. _____
3. _____

Today I mostly felt:

Draw how you felt on the unicorn's face

Did anything make me feel anxious, frustrated or sad? If so, why?

_____

_____

_____

_____

_____

Top three things about today:

(1) _____

(2) _____

(3) _____

Three things I'm grateful for today:

(1) _____

(2) _____

(3) _____

This is my work of art   Date: _____

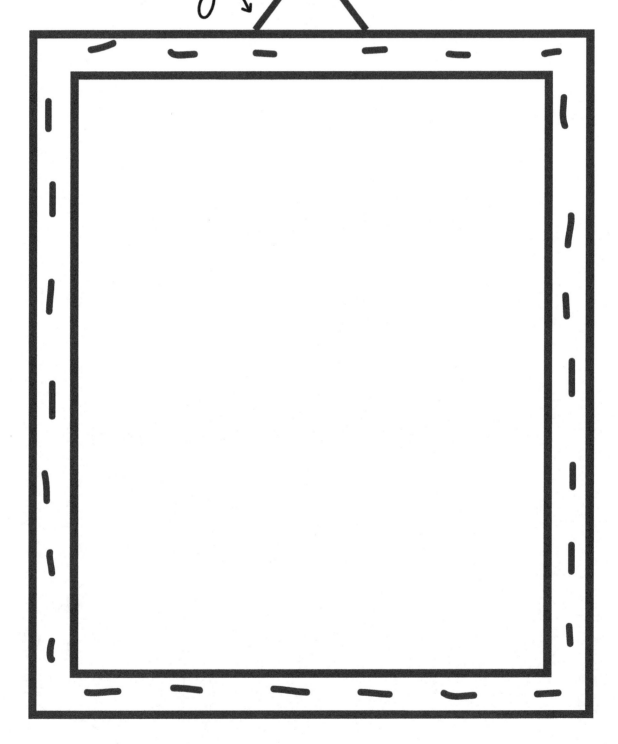

Date: _____

If you were granted 3 wishes what would they be?

M T W T F S S

Date: _____

Three things I felt today:

(1) _____
(2) _____
(3) _____

Today I mostly felt:

Draw how you felt on the unicorn's face

Did anything make me feel anxious, frustrated or sad? If so, why?

_____

_____

_____

_____

_____

Top three things about today:

1 _____

2 _____

3 _____

Three things I'm grateful for today:

1 _____

2 _____

3 _____

M T W T F S S

Date: _____

Three things I felt today:

① _____
② _____
③ _____

Today I mostly felt:

Draw how you felt on the unicorn's face

Did anything make me feel anxious, frustrated or sad? If so, why?

_____

_____

_____

_____

_____

Top three things about today:

① _____

② _____

③ _____

Three things I'm grateful for today:

① _____

② _____

③ _____

M T W T F S S

Date: _____

Three things I felt today:

① _____

② _____

③ _____

Today I mostly felt:

Draw how you felt on the unicorn's face

Did anything make me feel anxious, frustrated or sad? If so, why?

_____

_____

_____

_____

_____

Top three things about today:

① _____

② _____

③ _____

Three things I'm grateful for today:

① _____

② _____

③ _____

M T W T F S S

Date: _____

Three things I felt today:

1. _____
2. _____
3. _____

Today I mostly felt:

Draw how you felt on the unicorn's face

Did anything make me feel anxious, frustrated or sad? If so, why?

_____

_____

_____

_____

_____

Top three things about today:

① _____

② _____

③ _____

Three things I'm grateful for today:

① _____

② _____

③ _____

M T W T F S S

Date: _____

Three things I felt today:

① _____

② _____

③ _____

Today I mostly felt:

Draw how you felt on the unicorn's face

Did anything make me feel anxious, frustrated or sad? If so, why?

_____

_____

_____

_____

_____

Top three things about today:

1 _____

2 _____

3 _____

Three things I'm grateful for today:

1 _____

2 _____

3 _____

This is my work of art

Date: _____

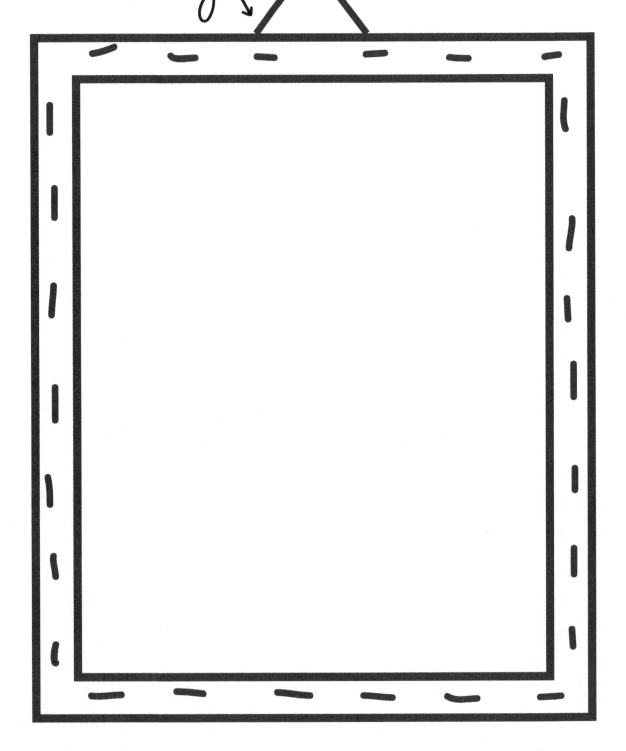

Date: _____

What is your greatest talent?

_____
_____
_____
_____
_____
_____
_____
_____
_____
_____
_____
_____
_____
_____
_____
_____
_____
_____

M T W T F S S

Date: _____

Three things I felt today:

 ①

 ②

 ③

Today I mostly felt:

😃 🙂

☹️ 😠

😢 😬

Draw how you felt on the unicorn's face ↱

Did anything make me feel anxious, frustrated or sad? If so, why?

_____

_____

_____

_____

_____

Top three things about today:

① _____

② _____

③ _____

Three things I'm grateful for today:

① _____

② _____

③ _____

M T W T F S S

Date: _____

Three things I felt today:

1. _____
2. _____
3. _____

Today I mostly felt:

Draw how you felt on the unicorn's face

Did anything make me feel anxious, frustrated or sad? If so, why?

_____

_____

_____

_____

_____

Top three things about today:

① _____

② _____

③ _____

Three things I'm grateful for today:

① _____

② _____

③ _____

M T W T F S S

Date: _____

Three things I felt today:

① _____

② _____

③ _____

Today I mostly felt:

Draw how you felt on the unicorn's face

Did anything make me feel anxious, frustrated or sad? If so, why?

_____

_____

_____

_____

_____

Top three things about today:

(1) _____

(2) _____

(3) _____

Three things I'm grateful for today:

(1) _____

(2) _____

(3) _____

M T W T F S S

Date: _____

Three things I felt today:

1. _____
2. _____
3. _____

Today I mostly felt:

Draw how you felt on the unicorn's face ↱

Did anything make me feel anxious, frustrated or sad? If so, why?

_____
_____
_____
_____
_____

Top three things about today:

1 _____
2 _____
3 _____

Three things I'm grateful for today:

1 _____
2 _____
3 _____

M T W T F S S

Date: _____

Three things I felt today:

1. _____
2. _____
3. _____

Today I mostly felt:

Draw how you felt on the unicorn's face

Did anything make me feel anxious, frustrated or sad? If so, why?

_____

_____

_____

_____

_____

Top three things about today:

① _____

② _____

③ _____

Three things I'm grateful for today:

① _____

② _____

③ _____

This is my work of art

Date: _____

Date: _____

Write about a time you felt nervous or anxious. What happened?

_____

_____

_____

_____

_____

_____

_____

_____

_____

_____

_____

_____

_____

_____

_____

_____

_____

_____

_____

_____

M T W T F S S

Date: _____

Three things I felt today:

① _____
② _____
③ _____

Today I mostly felt:

Draw how you felt on the unicorn's face

Did anything make me feel anxious, frustrated or sad? If so, why?

_____
_____
_____
_____
_____

Top three things about today:

1) _____
2) _____
3) _____

Three things I'm grateful for today:

1) _____
2) _____
3) _____

M T W T F S S

Date: _____

Three things I felt today:

1.
2.
3.

Today I mostly felt:

Draw how you felt on the unicorn's face

Did anything make me feel anxious, frustrated or sad? If so, why?

_____

_____

_____

_____

Top three things about today:

1. _____
2. _____
3. _____

Three things I'm grateful for today:

1. _____
2. _____
3. _____

M T W T F S S

Date: _____

Three things I felt today:

1. _____
2. _____
3. _____

Today I mostly felt:

Draw how you felt on the unicorn's face

Did anything make me feel anxious, frustrated or sad? If so, why?

_____

_____

_____

_____

Top three things about today:

1. _____
2. _____
3. _____

Three things I'm grateful for today:

1. _____
2. _____
3. _____

M T W T F S S

Date: _____

Three things I felt today:

1. _____
2. _____
3. _____

Today I mostly felt:

Draw how you felt on the unicorn's face

Did anything make me feel anxious, frustrated or sad? If so, why?

_____

_____

_____

_____

_____

Top three things about today:

① _____

② _____

③ _____

Three things I'm grateful for today:

① _____

② _____

③ _____

M T W T F S S

Date: _____

Three things I felt today:

 1
2
3

Today I mostly felt:

Draw how you felt on the unicorn's face

Did anything make me feel anxious, frustrated or sad? If so, why?

_____

_____

_____

_____

_____

Top three things about today:

① _____

② _____

③ _____

Three things I'm grateful for today:

① _____

② _____

③ _____

This is my work of art   Date: _____

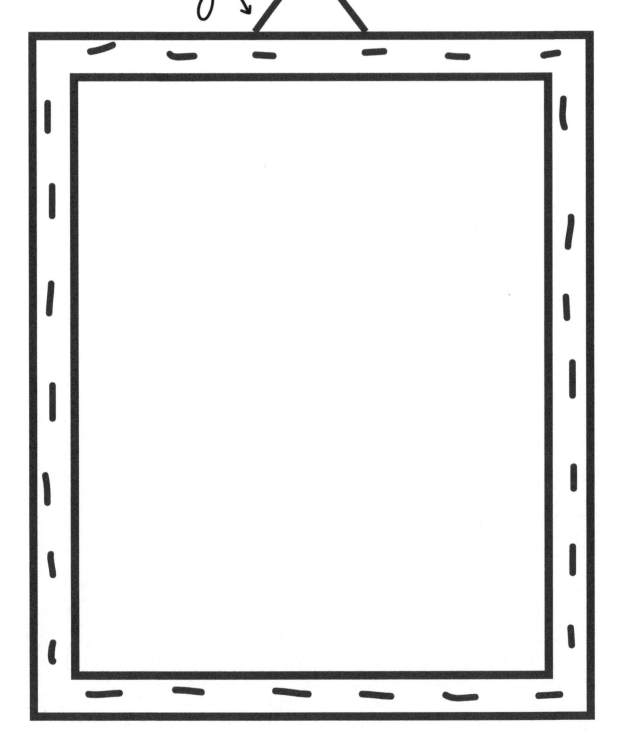

Date: _____

Write about a time someone made you feel good about yourself.

_____

_____

_____

_____

_____

_____

_____

_____

_____

_____

_____

_____

_____

_____

_____

_____

_____

_____

MTWTFSS

Date: _____

Three things I felt today:

1. _____
2. _____
3. _____

Today I mostly felt:

Draw how you felt on the unicorn's face

Did anything make me feel anxious, frustrated or sad? If so, why?

_____

_____

_____

_____

Top three things about today:

(1) _____

(2) _____

(3) _____

Three things I'm grateful for today:

(1) _____

(2) _____

(3) _____

M T W T F S S

Date: _____

Three things I felt today:

① _____
② _____
③ _____

Today I mostly felt:

Draw how you felt on the unicorn's face

Did anything make me feel anxious, frustrated or sad? If so, why?

_____

_____

_____

_____

_____

Top three things about today:

(1) _____

(2) _____

(3) _____

Three things I'm grateful for today:

(1) _____

(2) _____

(3) _____

M T W T F S S

Date: _____

Three things I felt today:

① _____
② _____
③ _____

Today I mostly felt:

Draw how you felt on the unicorn's face

Did anything make me feel anxious, frustrated or sad? If so, why?

_____

_____

_____

_____

Top three things about today:

① _____

② _____

③ _____

Three things I'm grateful for today:

① _____

② _____

③ _____

M T W T F S S

Date: _____

Three things I felt today:

1. _____
2. _____
3. _____

Today I mostly felt:

Draw how you felt on the unicorn's face

Did anything make me feel anxious, frustrated or sad? If so, why?

_____

_____

_____

_____

_____

Top three things about today:

① _____

② _____

③ _____

Three things I'm grateful for today:

① _____

② _____

③ _____

M T W T F S S

Date: _____

Three things I felt today:

① _____
② _____
③ _____

Today I mostly felt:

Draw how you felt on the unicorn's face

Did anything make me feel anxious, frustrated or sad? If so, why?

Top three things about today:

1
2
3

Three things I'm grateful for today:

1
2
3

This is my work of art

Date: _____

Date: _____

What age are you most looking forward to in the future?

_____
_____
_____
_____
_____
_____
_____
_____
_____
_____
_____
_____
_____
_____
_____
_____
_____
_____
_____
_____

M T W T F S S

Date: _____

Three things I felt today:

1.
2.
3.

Today I mostly felt:

Draw how you felt on the unicorn's face →

Did anything make me feel anxious, frustrated or sad? If so, why?

_____

_____

_____

_____

Top three things about today:

1 _____

2 _____

3 _____

Three things I'm grateful for today:

1 _____

2 _____

3 _____

M T W T F S S

Date: _____

Three things I felt today:

1. _____
2. _____
3. _____

Today I mostly felt:

Draw how you felt on the unicorn's face

Did anything make me feel anxious, frustrated or sad? If so, why?

_____

_____

_____

_____

_____

Top three things about today:

(1) _____

(2) _____

(3) _____

Three things I'm grateful for today:

(1) _____

(2) _____

(3) _____

M T W T F S S

Date: _____

Three things I felt today:

1 _____
2 _____
3 _____

Today I mostly felt:

Draw how you felt on the unicorn's face

Did anything make me feel anxious, frustrated or sad? If so, why?

_____

_____

_____

_____

Top three things about today:

① _____

② _____

③ _____

Three things I'm grateful for today:

① _____

② _____

③ _____

M T W T F S S

Date: _____

Three things I felt today:

1. _____
2. _____
3. _____

Today I mostly felt:

Draw how you felt on the unicorn's face

Did anything make me feel anxious, frustrated or sad? If so, why?

_____

_____

_____

_____

_____

Top three things about today:

① _____

② _____

③ _____

Three things I'm grateful for today:

① _____

② _____

③ _____

M T W T F S S

Date: _____

Three things I felt today:

1. _____
2. _____
3. _____

Today I mostly felt:

Draw how you felt on the unicorn's face

Did anything make me feel anxious, frustrated or sad? If so, why?

_____

_____

_____

_____

_____

Top three things about today:

① _____

② _____

③ _____

Three things I'm grateful for today:

① _____

② _____

③ _____

This is my work of art

Date: _____

Date: _____

What is the most interesting thing you've ever done?

_____

_____

_____

_____

_____

_____

_____

_____

_____

_____

_____

_____

_____

_____

_____

_____

_____

_____

_____

M T W T F S S

Date: _____

Three things I felt today:

1
2
3

Today I mostly felt:

Draw how you felt on the unicorn's face

Did anything make me feel anxious, frustrated or sad? If so, why?

_____
_____
_____
_____
_____

Top three things about today:

① _____
② _____
③ _____

Three things I'm grateful for today:

① _____
② _____
③ _____

M T W T F S S

Date: _____

Three things I felt today:

① _____

② _____

③ _____

Today I mostly felt:

Draw how you felt on the unicorn's face

Did anything make me feel anxious, frustrated or sad? If so, why?

_____
_____
_____
_____
_____

Top three things about today:

1 _____
2 _____
3 _____

Three things I'm grateful for today:

1 _____
2 _____
3 _____

M T W T F S S

Date: _____

Three things I felt today:

1 _____

2 _____

3 _____

Today I mostly felt:

Draw how you felt on the unicorn's face

Did anything make me feel anxious, frustrated or sad? If so, why?

_____

_____

_____

_____

_____

Top three things about today:

1. _____

2. _____

3. _____

Three things I'm grateful for today:

1. _____

2. _____

3. _____

M T W T F S S

Date: _____

Three things I felt today:

1 _____
2 _____
3 _____

Today I mostly felt:

Draw how you felt on the unicorn's face

Did anything make me feel anxious, frustrated or sad? If so, why?

_____

_____

_____

_____

_____

Top three things about today:

1 _____

2 _____

3 _____

Three things I'm grateful for today:

1 _____

2 _____

3 _____

This is my work of art   Date: _____

Date: _____

If you could be a superhero what special powers would you choose?

_____
_____
_____
_____
_____
_____
_____
_____
_____
_____
_____
_____
_____
_____
_____
_____
_____
_____
_____
_____
_____

If you like this book, please give us a positive rating and review on Amazon - it means a lot! Scan below to go to the book review page.

Made in the USA
Columbia, SC
12 April 2022

58861106R00063